Creative Teaching on a Budget

Janet K. Tipton
Purdue University

Merrill,
an imprint of Prentice Hall
Upper Saddle River, New Jersey   *Columbus, Ohio*

**For Brad and Joy,
my inspiration.**

Editor: Debra A. Stollenwerk
Production Editor: JoEllen Gohr
Cover Designer: Diane C. Lorenzo
Cover Art: © Photodisk, Inc.
Production Manager: Pamela Bennett
Director of Marketing: Kevin Flanagan
Marketing Manager: Suzanne Stanton
Marketing Coordinator: Krista Groshong

Printed in the United States of America

10 9 8

ISBN: 0-13-084715-1

TABLE OF CONTENTS

INTRODUCTION

Teachers at all levels, particularly elementary school teachers, often spend their own money to buy things they need for teaching that the school does not provide. Many teachers have resigned themselves to the fact that this just "goes with the territory," while others have learned to be resourceful scavengers.

If you want to be a teacher who really takes home most of your take-home pay, and still offers interesting and exciting lessons for your students, read on. This book presents many ideas for creative lessons that will require little or no expenditure of your personal funds. You can provide interesting, exciting lessons inexpensively.

The first thing you need to do is to look at each situation with new eyes. As you prepare to discard an item, ask yourself if it can be given new life in some type of project at school. Many items you may have placed in your recycling bin can be reused for something else.

Do not stop with just looking at items you were going to discard at home. When you go into a store and see a catchy display that could be adapted for use in your classroom, ask the manager if you might have it at the end of the particular promotion. The display might be thrown away anyway.

Be aware of agencies in your community that may offer free or inexpensive services or materials that will be useful in your classroom. Also be aware of the rules of "fair use" when it comes to sharing things from TV or the Internet with your class.

We have all heard stories of—or perhaps observed firsthand—a child who opens a present and tosses the gift aside to play with the box. The message for teachers here is that our students do not require that we spend lots of our own money buying things that attract and entertain them. The real pleasure in learning is the creativity one can discover within himself or herself. This book offers many examples of inexpensive or free materials you can obtain and use to create exciting lessons for your students. Once you try a few of these ideas, you are sure to discover many more of your own. At this point you will truly become a creative teacher.

PART I

COMMUNITY RESOURCES

Numerous resources exist in and around your community that will help you teach creatively, yet inexpensively. You can find many of these resources by recycling or adapting items that might be discarded or otherwise unused. In addition, you will want to enlist the help of businesses and parents because they are invaluable resources.

CHAPTER 1
REDUCE, REUSE, RECYCLE

Like many Americans, you may have become accustomed to recycling. It is not unusual for a typical household to recycle two to three times as much material as it discards as trash. This makes us feel that we are doing our part to help the environment. However, many of the materials marked for recycling can be reused for another purpose. Let's look at some ideas for reusing those items.

Plastic Items

Small plastic containers with lids such as **yogurt or margarine containers** can be used for water pans for painting, containers to hold small loose items such as paper clips, tacks, corn, beans, etc. **Larger margarine containers** are useful for storing items such as pieces of crayon, chalk, markers, game pieces, etc. **Containers for 35-mm film** are handy for storing small odds and ends. For younger students, these make excellent containers in which to put various items, with distinctive smells for students to identify. Empty **prescription bottles** in a variety of sizes can be used for storage, for stacking, or in art projects. Be sure to remove the prescription labels. It might be a good idea to spray paint these bottles so they don't look so much like medicine bottles. At any rate, if you use prescription bottles, be sure your students understand that it is not OK to take and play with these bottles from medicine cabinets at home.

    All sizes and types of empty containers can be used in student art projects such as building model towns, forts, castles, space stations, etc. **Strawberry boxes** made of plastic make perfect, inexpensive baskets for Easter or May Day creations. There are also many uses for **two-liter soft drink bottles**. A knife will easily cut these bottles so they can be fashioned into terrariums, splash guards for large drink dispensers, or baskets for any occasion. **One-gallon plastic jugs** joined together with string, wire, glue, and/or tape make a life-sized igloo for younger children to explore. These may also be used in the same ways as the two-liter bottles when a larger size is desired.

Cardboard Items

Cardboard pieces of all shapes and sizes have numerous uses. **Large appliance boxes** make wonderful props and backgrounds for students' plays. Tempera paint works very well on cardboard; it is inexpensive, easily cleaned, and readily available in most schools. These larger boxes are also useful when cut into three-sided display boards for student projects such as science fair displays. Again, the cardboard may be painted or covered with construction paper or fabric for an attractive, low-cost display. One side of a large box makes a nice substitute for a piece of poster board. Encourage students to seek these inexpensive alternatives to ready-made poster board or display boards; it will allow them to feel a sense of pride in their creativity and resourcefulness when they transform an old box into an attractive display.

      Packing materials inside computer boxes are often quite useful. A recent trip to the trash bin outside of school yielded a gold mine because the school had bought a room full of new computers. Each box had packed inside a large, flat piece of cardboard with a handle, two substantial pieces of Styrofoam, and a small, flat cardboard box. From the large, flat cardboard pieces and Styrofoam, it was possible to make study carrels to serve as dividers during testing. The smaller, flat box worked well for student portfolios. **Pizza boxes** also make nice student portfolio boxes; they allow room for items that are not the usual 8 1/2- by 11-inch flat pieces of paper, such as videotapes or audiotapes and art projects.

      Cereal and cracker boxes have many uses (see Cereal Box Unit lesson plan in Part II). The boxes themselves are useful in lessons on nutrition as students can study the ingredients listed. They also are particularly useful in studying advertising techniques. After you finish using the outside of the boxes for various lessons, they make great storage units for a variety of things. For short-term student projects, they can be covered with construction paper. For long-term storage, contact paper will make a cereal box into a durable container (see Packaging Your Portfolio lesson plan in Part II).

Smaller pieces of cardboard, such as tablet backs or the type used in packing shirts, are also very useful. These make good platforms for small student models, such as sugar-cube igloos. Student artwork that is to be saved for a portfolio or displayed on the wall can be mounted on these pieces of cardboard with rubber cement.

Paper towel and toilet paper rolls find new roles as columns for a Greek temple or logs in a log cabin for student-built models. Your students undoubtedly will use their imaginations to discover many more uses for these cardboard cylinders.

Other Miscellaneous Items Saved from the Trash

Small items such as bottle caps and buttons work well for counting activities for young children. They are also useful for sorting and classifying (see Classification lesson plan in Part II). A variety of objects will add interest to these lessons.

When the new year arrives, save old wall calendars. Pictures from wall calendars are very useful in the classroom. Cut the calendars apart, trim neatly, then laminate the pictures. These pictures can be used as story starters for creative writing. When working on descriptive writing, students can write a description of the pictures. You can display all of the pictures in the front of the room, give each student a description written by another student, and see if they can match the description with the picture. These laminated calendar pictures can be used over and over again in a variety of activities, and they will last for several years.

You can also add to your picture file by collecting interesting pictures from magazines or outdated textbooks that are to be discarded. Again, trim the pictures and laminate them. As you add to this file and you have too many pictures to put in a file folder, organize them by subject matter in cardboard pizza boxes. These boxes will stack neatly and can accommodate pictures of different sizes.

Do not forget to provide a box near the computer both at home and at school for paper that is used only on one side. Students should

10

form the habit of printing drafts of documents on recycled paper. Then when they have done their editing and made necessary changes, they can use a clean sheet of paper for their final copy. You will be amazed at how much paper can be saved this way.

CHAPTER 2
IDEAS FROM THE SUPERMARKET

Many ordinary items that are available at the supermarket can be used in lessons. If you plan ahead, you might be able to recruit parents to pick up an extra item or two for use in your classroom when they do their grocery shopping. Add some variety to your lessons by trying several of these ideas.

Painting

It is not always necessary to obtain special paper for painting projects. **Brown paper grocery bags** and pieces of **cardboard** are suitable for most types of painting. In some cases, these materials are even superior to traditional painting paper. The brown paper bags make good substitutes for bark, animal skins, or papyrus in Australian Aboriginal, Native American, or Ancient Egyptian paintings.

Give your students some variety by using nontraditional substitutes for paint. **Food coloring** can be used in place of watercolors. **Liquid shoe polish** makes good paint, and the dauber in the bottle makes an interesting brush. **Colored chalk** used on damp paper will dry to look like paint as it soaks into the paper.

Finger paint can be made by adding powdered tempera paint to **liquid starch.** As a special treat for younger children, make finger paints with **instant pudding.** Use the vanilla flavor and then add food coloring to make the various colors. Students can lick their fingers when they finish painting. (Make sure you explain to students that this is a *special* kind of finger paint and that they should never eat regular paint!) Let the students help make the pudding. Put the instant pudding mix, milk, and food coloring in a sealed plastic container, then have students take turns shaking the container until pudding is set. They will enjoy the process and have a better understanding of the fact that it is really food.

Children will enjoy painting with a **variety of tools.** Save the expensive paintbrushes for older students. Unleash their creativity by allowing them to paint with **cotton swabs, cotton balls, toothbrushes, sponges, and combs**. These tools will allow them to make some interesting textures. Students can also create an interesting effect by dropping a small amount of paint on the paper and then blowing through a **drinking straw** to move it around to create their design.

Printing

You can make interesting prints by converting various items into "print plates," dipping them in paint, and then applying the plates to a surface. Use various **vegetables and fruits** to make plates. Pieces of **cabbage** or **onions,** cut across the grain to form a pattern, make attractive circular prints. Cut **potatoes** in half and carve a design onto the flat side to be used for printing. Ears of **corn** can be used with the corn on or off for printing. Put corn holders in each end of the ear and roll it across your paper. **Carrots, turnips**, and **green peppers** also make nice print designs. **Citrus fruits** may need to be blotted to eliminate excess juice. After dipping the plates in paint, be sure to blot them with paper towels before applying to surfaces.

Other nonedible items from the supermarket also may be used for printing. Several thicknesses of **paper towels** placed in a **Styrofoam meat tray** can be used for a print pad. Use a different pad for each color of paint you wish to use. Discard the pads when you are finished printing.

A **bar of soap** can be carved with any design and used to make prints. **Sponges** cut into various shapes also make good printing tools. Use rubber cement to cover a **cardboard roll** from toilet paper or paper towels with **string** or **yarn** to make a roller; it will make lines on your paper for an interesting textured effect.

Plates can be made for prints you wish to use repeatedly; e.g., for students' holiday greeting cards. Take a **Styrofoam meat tray** and trim the edges so it is completely flat. Use glue to make the design on the Styrofoam. (Remember that any wording will need to be drawn backwards so it will print correctly on the surface. Have students practice this on paper first, then hold the paper in front of a mirror to see if it is correct.) After the design dries, use it to print the cards. Achieve a similar effect by using a piece of **cardboard** and gluing **yarn** in your desired design.

Students can print designs on plain **tissue paper,** either white or colored, to make very attractive gift wrap. If they are making a gift at school for their parents, they can make their own gift wrap and take the present home already wrapped. The same motif can be repeated on a greeting card for a professional look that will make students very proud of their gift and its wrapping.

Miscellaneous Art Projects

Melt–Art

When **crayons** break or get too small for students to use easily, they still have use in melt–art. Crayon pieces can be scraped into shavings with a **cheese grater.** Keep different colors in **Ziploc bags** to keep them separate. Have students make **waxed paper** pictures by arranging the crayon shavings on one piece of waxed paper in the desired pattern. Carefully place another piece of waxed paper on top of the crayon shavings. Put a piece of **aluminum foil** over the picture, and press it with a warm iron. The crayon pieces will melt and make a lovely effect. The finished artwork could be displayed on the classroom windows to create a stained glass effect. You can use this technique to make placemats by matting the melt–art picture with construction paper.

Sculptures

Use bars of **soap** or blocks of **paraffin** for sculptures. Students can experiment with a variety of **kitchen utensils** to create texture.

Clay

Modeling **clay** is simple to make with ordinary kitchen ingredients. One method is to mix two parts **flour** to one part **salt** with just enough water to make it moldable. Another method combines one part **cornstarch,** one part cold water, and three parts **salt**. Add dried **tempera paint** or **food coloring** to make different colors with either mixture.

Fun with Food

Apples

Have your students test their own powers of observation. Give each student an **apple** or have students bring one from home. Tell students to spend a few minutes closely observing their apples, taking notes if they wish. Then have them turn their apples in to you. As students turn them in, put a stick-on number on each apple and record the students' corresponding names. Randomly assign the numbers so no patterns might be detected, and do not let students see the numbers you assign to the apples. After all apples are labeled, put them in a bag. Then spread a clean towel on the floor, and empty the sack of apples onto the towel. See if students can identify their own apples. When everyone is content that they have found their own, read the number list aloud to see how well students did. If you allow students to bring apples from home, you may have several different varieties of apples; this will make it easier for students to identify their own apples. If you purchase a bag of just one kind of apple, the exercise will be more challenging for students.

Pumpkins

Pumpkins are usually plentiful in the fall, and you may be able to obtain them very cheaply in early November. Besides the normal fall activities with pumpkins, they are also useful in teaching about maps and globes. It is preferable to have one pumpkin for each student, but if that is not possible, try to have at least enough that students can work in small groups of two or three. Depending on the age of students, you may need to do the actual carving.

Have students use **colored string or thread** to mark the lines of latitude and longitude. With younger students, you may only want to mark the Equator and Prime Meridian. Older students can label more lines. Run the string or thread through **white school glue** to make it stick to the pumpkin, and hold the ends in place with **straight pins**. The glue will be clear when it dries.

After labeling is done and the pumpkins have been used for any lesson illustrations needed, according to grade level, it is time to carve them. On one pumpkin, try to cut along the Equator, so that you can illustrate the Northern and Southern Hemispheres. On another pumpkin, slice it in half at the Prime Meridian, illustrating Eastern and Western Hemispheres. Clean the inside of the pumpkins. Have students attempt to cut their pumpkins in such a way that the pieces will lie flat to make a map. You then will be able to illustrate map distortion.

With very young children, it might be best for the teacher to just demonstrate these concepts with one or two pumpkins. Older students can be taught about degrees in a circle, and they can practice measuring and marking the lines of latitude and longitude in the proper scale.

Eggs

A couple dozen **eggs** can go a long way in a creative teacher's classroom. Ask students to bring in eggs, or pick them up yourself at the store.

The first activity is to have students plan and build protective **egg containers** to protect eggs from a fall of several feet. You can make up your own rules for this contest—offer only specific materials the students can use, or let them bring in any materials they like. You may want to specify a maximum size allowed for the egg containers. After containers are built, take the class to the designated drop-off point for the experiment. The drop-off point should be at least a couple of stories high and end on a hard surface. One by one, drop the egg-filled containers. The designers of the cartons that protected the eggs from breaking will be the winners of the contest.

Use remaining unbroken eggs or use a new dozen or two for different methods of hard-boiling eggs. Bring in, or have students bring in, several different cookbooks. Arrange students into groups and have them try the different methods of boiling eggs explained in the cookbooks. After the experiment, students can break open the eggs to see to what degree they became hard-boiled. Were the eggs that were boiled for only eight minutes as hard (or "done") as those that were boiled for twenty minutes? Can you boil the eggs too long? How can you tell?

The last activity is an experiment in **natural dyes**. It can fit in well with studying almost any early civilization, and it will also be appropriate in a unit on early American pioneer life. Ask students to hypothesize what materials early people used to make natural vegetable dyes. Then try making some natural dyes and coloring the hard-boiled eggs from the last activity. Beet juice, onionskins, and carrot tops all make good natural dyes. You and your students may come up with other materials as well—just be sure they are edible substances. Onionskins and carrot tops can be boiled for a few minutes in some water, and beet juice can be used as is. Students may recall which fruits or vegetables stained their hands; perhaps some of these will be suitable for dyes.

Mosaics

Clean your cupboard at home (and ask parents to do the same), and bring in all the little bits of leftover **macaroni, rice, dried beans,** etc. Pop a batch of **popcorn**. Now allow students to use these materials to create mosaic pictures on pieces of cardboard, using a glue that is transparent when it dries.

Space Pudding

As a culminating activity for a unit on space, have students make and eat space pudding. Simply mix **instant pudding** and put single servings into **Ziploc sandwich bags**. To simulate eating in space, have students snip one corner of the sandwich bags with scissors and then squeeze the pudding into their mouths.

CHAPTER 3
NEWSPAPERS

Your local newspaper can provide for numerous creative lessons for your students. The first thing you need to do is to check to see if there is a Newspaper in Education Editor at your local paper. This person is your contact person for many newspaper resources, starting with getting the newspaper delivered to your classroom. Often the newspaper has a list of businesses that will donate the cost of the newspaper for your classroom. You may, however, need to find your own sponsor.

Once you have established contact with the NIE Editor and have arranged for delivery of newspapers to your classroom on a regular basis, you will have to determine just how you plan to use the newspapers. Check with the NIE Editor for free resource guides the newspaper provides. The guides are full of lesson plans and ideas for using the newspaper in your classroom.

Usually there is a special week in the spring designated as NIE Week, when even more resources are available. It may include information on a free workshop you might attend or, at least, a new booklet of ideas.

A TYPICAL WEEK USING THE NEWSPAPER

To get you started, let's take a look at a typical week using the newspaper in a middle grade classroom.

Tuesday

A classroom set of newspapers is delivered to your classroom. That morning, students read the paper, concentrating on world news in the front section. After fifteen to twenty minutes of reading time, a current events discussion is held on topics students choose from the paper. Free reading time is then provided so students may read the remaining sections of the paper as they choose. They may also read the special section for students, which discusses topics of interest to them. They may review and respond to the poll that this section includes, the results of which will appear in next week's student section.

Wednesday

The students take a current events quiz containing information from yesterday's paper. Students use randomly selected, cutout headlines as starters for stories they will write. Younger students could use comic strips in which the dialogue has been marked out with correction fluid in order to write their own dialogue.

Thursday

A discussion of editorial cartoons is held using political cartoons from the current and previous weeks' papers as examples. The students then create their own political cartoons on topics relevant to them, such as school lunches, dress code, and the like.

Friday

The students pick up imprints from the comic section with silly putty to illustrate map distortion. (Start with a round ball of putty, press it onto paper to pick up imprint, then try to flatten it without distorting the picture.)

Monday

The following Monday, students make papier-mâché globes from newspaper as a follow-up to the map distortion lesson on Friday. You can use leftover pages from the newspaper to create a background for a current events bulletin board. Recycle any remaining parts of the newspaper before the next set of papers is delivered tomorrow.

OTHER IDEAS

These are just a few ideas for using the newspaper in your classroom. These suggestions may be modified for younger or older students. Middle school or high school students might spend more time with current events and reading the editorial page. They could even be encouraged to write letters to the editor on a local issue affecting them. Younger students might circle all the verbs, nouns, or pronouns on a given page as part of a language lesson. Once you get started using the newspaper, you will undoubtedly come up with your own creative ideas. Don't forget to contact your local paper for the NIE resources available to you as well.

CHAPTER 4
BUSINESS PARTNERSHIPS

More and more, businesses are interested in becoming involved in education. Some schools already have business partners in education. A school can realize many advantages from such a relationship.

For many years businesses have been asked to **sponsor** a softball team or to **buy advertising** in school yearbooks or sports programs. This, however, is a rather one-sided way that businesses may be involved in education and really amounts to just asking for money.

Many businesses are now interested in taking a more active role in education. Some employers promote the idea of their employees acting as **mentors** and even give them some time off work each week to go to the school to work with students. This regular contact with a positive adult role model can be beneficial for students, and the extra attention students receive helps offset the effects of large class size.

It might be effective to have **speakers** come talk to your class about their businesses. This is particularly useful in career education.

Businesses that Recycle

Banks, large corporations, and even doctors tend to redecorate their offices on a regular basis. Once you establish a business partnership, let your partner know that you would be interested in taking some of its **used office furniture** when it is no longer needed. You may discover a gold mine of very usable items, such as desks, chairs, bookcases, file cabinets, and tables.

Let your partner know that you are also interested in **small office supplies.** **Three-ring binders** are often leftover from conferences or special promotions that are no longer needed by the business and can be used in your classroom. You may also use boxes of **letterhead** that are no longer used because some information is no longer correct. Students can use this paper to print draft copies of their work. Your business partner can probably provide you with more useful items for your classroom that are no longer needed at the business.

Home Decorating Businesses

Stores that specialize in items for home decoration may provide many items that you can use in your classroom. Outdated **wallpaper catalogs** provide wonderful material for all sorts of classroom artwork. These pieces of wallpaper can be used for many things such as portfolio covers, greeting cards, bulletin boards, wallcovering for model buildings, and collages.

Carpet companies also discontinue certain styles of carpeting, so **carpet samples** become obsolete. They can still have a new life in your classroom. As is, they can be used as mats for students to sit or lie upon the floor. Several pieces can be joined to form an attractive patchwork quilt effect in the room for a reading corner. These carpet samples can also be attached to the walls to minimize noise and give the area a warm and cozy effect. When cut into smaller pieces, the carpet can be used in models the students build.

Restaurants

Restaurants can also be a source of materials for many creative lessons. Students can use **outdated menus** to role-play going to a restaurant to order dinner. If the lesson is on nutrition, have students choose a well-balanced meal. If it is a math lesson, have them determine what they can afford on a budget.

Fast-food restaurants often have **promotional materials** that use movie cartoon characters with which your students will be familiar. Or when you see store decorations that might be used in your classroom, ask the manager if you might have them when the promotion ends. Many times these materials are just thrown away after the promotion. In addition, the **small prizes** that accompany these promotions can be used for incentives, rewards, or game prizes in your classroom or as items students might buy with play money.

Of course, don't forget the ever-useful **pizza boxes**. You can collect these at home as you use them, or ask at pizza restaurants for new boxes for special projects.

CHAPTER 5
FIELD TRIP ALTERNATIVES

Field trips can be wonderful teaching tools that connect students' learning with real-world experiences. However, in the days of downsizing and budget cutting, field trips may be one of the first things to be cut from the school budget. Although there may not be a perfect replacement for some field trips that seem essential to learning certain things, this chapter offers some alternatives to field trips that you might want to consider.

Speakers

Many agencies will provide speakers at no charge to visit your classroom. For example, instead of a trip to the zoo, perhaps a representative from the zoo will come to your classroom and even bring a few small animals for the students to observe. A speaker from the local newspaper could come in to explain how the paper is prepared and bring in some proof copies or paste-ups for students to view. A local banker could come in to speak to students about savings accounts or another appropriate topic for their level.

Check with your local chamber of commerce to see if they have a speaker's bureau. It may have a list of business people from the community who are prepared to come speak to your class. In fact, this list may give you ideas for lessons that you had not previously considered.

Teacher-Taped "Field Trips"

If just having a speaker come in to talk to your class doesn't seem like a good substitute for a field trip—perhaps there are things at the site that they should see—you might go on the field trip by yourself and videotape the experience. Plan carefully for a quality video that will hold your students' attention. If you have visited the site before, write a list of the things you want to videotape and the points you want to make. If you have never been there, you might need to make two visits—one to experience it for yourself and the second to actually make the video. Write a script, or at least an outline, so you will not forget to mention anything important. If possible, have someone else do the videotaping, so you can concentrate on the script and perhaps even be shown in the video.

Virtual Field Trips

Virtual field trips may be the wave of the future. Through audio-video hookups, students can view the site and ask questions of the site experts. Several of these sites are already in operation. It may be cost-prohibitive for your school to set up such a hookup, but you may be able to tap into one that is already established. Students could also visit interactive Web sites for a virtual field trip. (See Part III for Web sites.)

A conference call is a cheaper alternative to the audio-video hookup. At a prearranged time, a phone call is made from the classroom to an expert the students wish to interview. The students prepare questions ahead of time and use a speakerphone in the classroom to ask the questions of the interviewee. This is less desirable than the audio-video connection but is very effective in some cases.

Walking Field Trips

The major expenditure for many field trips is the cost of the bus and bus driver. A way to eliminate that expense is to take a field trip on foot. Most schools are in walking distance from some interesting sites. Depending on the level of the students, grocery store visits or visits to governmental offices can be extensions of their schoolwork. (See Cemetery Study and Study Plots lesson plans in Part II.)

Public Transportation

In some cities, students may use city buses at no charge. Check with your local city bus company about student rates. If bus routes are easily accessible and will take you close to your destination, this could be a much more economical way of taking a field trip than using a school bus. You might want to consider including a lesson about using public transportation that will coincide with your field trip.

CHAPTER 6
INEXPENSIVE, LEGAL USE OF MEDIA

Building a Classroom Library

It is relatively easy to develop a classroom library of books for your students to use and enjoy without using your own funds. Public libraries are always purchasing new titles, so they need to dispose of some books in order to make room for the new ones. Contact your local public library to find the time of year when they dispose of old books. Some libraries sell books they need to discard for a few cents each or even give them away free. Magazines, including *National Geographic*, are also weeded out periodically. Even out-of-date magazines can be a great source of pictures for your picture file and be of value from a historical perspective.

Your school librarian may also periodically discard books, so be sure to check to see if you can use any of these in your classroom. Also, be on the lookout for teachers who are retiring and might want to leave their classroom library to you.

Your participation in paperback book clubs at school, such as Troll or Scholastic, also provides an avenue for free books for your classroom. For every book students order, you will earn bonus points that can be used to "purchase" books. These points can add up very quickly. Use them to purchase a class set of novels or individual titles to put in your classroom library.

If your students enjoy reading the books from your classroom library, you might be able to persuade them to donate to it. They may have used, unused, or unwanted books at home that they could donate to your classroom library. Depending on the resources available to your students, they might enjoy buying an extra book when they place their book orders and then donate it to your classroom library. One teacher even chose a novel she wanted to discuss in class, asked the students to buy their own copies, and then asked them to consider donating the books to the room library when they were finished with them. Keep in mind that when students donate books, they will enjoy writing "Donated by (their name)" in the front of the book.

Taping Programs from TV

Since the advent of VCRs and videotape, there has been confusion in the academic community concerning what is and is not legal to tape and use in the classroom. You can legally use programs or parts of programs taped from television in many ways. The fair-use provision of the Copyright Act allows reproduction and other uses of copyrighted works under certain conditions for purposes such as teaching (including multiple copies for classroom use). As more information becomes available only in electronic formats, the public's right of fair use extends to these formats. Teachers can expect to be able to use taped programs for legitimate teaching purposes without fear of violating copyright laws. For more information on this topic, see the following Web site: http://www.arl.cni.org/scomm/copyright/uses.html.

Borrowing Videotapes

Your school may have an arrangement with a central media distribution center for videotape loans. If you are part of a large school district, the district may even have its own media services division. Either way, these tapes are available for you to use in your classroom at no cost to you. You can be assured that videotapes from these services are legal to use in your classroom. Delivery and pick-up services may also be available, so all you have to do is reserve the tapes.

Some independent firms may also offer videotapes on a free loan basis. You will want to screen these carefully to be sure they are not blatantly advertising something (e.g., a film on nutrition from the National Dairy Council). However, most of these are acceptable. Availability of these films could be a problem. However, some agencies will send you videotapes that you can keep. This gives you more flexibility in scheduling when you will use them.

CHAPTER 7
PARENT HELP

Parents can be a great resource in your classroom, and allowing them the opportunity to help with their children's education can build valuable bridges with families. Parents may be involved in many different ways.

Make it a habit to find out early in the year the occupation of your students' parents. Then try to use the parents, if they are available, as guest speakers in your classroom whenever you can. This will yield many positive outcomes.

- It gives children a chance to feel proud of their parents.
- It gives parents a chance to "shine" in front of their children.
- It allows students to learn something from experts in different fields of study instead of from a book or from the teacher.
- It promotes the idea that we all, not just teachers, must be involved in the process of the educating our children.

Parents who may not want to or are not able to speak to the class about their jobs may be willing to volunteer help in a variety of other ways. This can include grading papers, accompanying students on field trips, or just being an "extra pair of hands" for a special activity.

All parents should be able to help collect recyclables for classroom use. Prepare a list of items you will need to collect for various class projects. Send it home with students at the beginning of the year and then throughout the year. You may be surprised at how quickly you will collect these items. In addition to the items already mentioned in Chapter 1, parents may be able to donate material scraps, felt scraps, fabric trim, and more.

Remember that parents can be excellent contacts when establishing business partners. Businesses may be more willing to get involved with your class if there is a special connection, such as a parent/employee. Parents can also be on the lookout for any items their businesses may be discarding that you can use in the classroom.

PART II

INTERDISCIPLINARY LESSON PLANS

This section contains a variety of lesson plans that are creative without requiring large expenditures on materials. They are listed by suggested grade level, but most lessons can be adapted to younger or older students. Most of the lessons are interdisciplinary; that is, they incorporate more than one subject area. They are listed by major subject area along with references to possible complementary areas.

CHAPTER 8
MATHEMATICS

Bottle Cap Math

Grade Level   K–2
Related Subjects   NA
Materials
- Assorted bottle caps
- Paper and pencils

Objective   Students will demonstrate counting, grouping, and regrouping with bottle caps.

Procedure   This activity may be done with students working individually or in groups of two or three.

Give students a container (three-pound coffee can or similar container) filled with assorted bottle caps. Have students count aloud each bottle cap as they remove it from the container and place it on a table or on the floor.

Next, have students group the bottle caps by twos, threes, fives, and tens. More advanced students can count how many groups they have each time and be shown how this becomes a multiplication problem. You can then have these students write the multiplication problem they have created by their grouping.

Students will write simple subtraction problems on paper and then have another student in the group illustrate the problems using bottle caps.

Students learning to regroup for subtraction will now group their bottle caps by tens. The teacher will illustrate how borrowing from the column on the left actually regroups by tens. Students will now practice writing problems using regrouping and then illustrate the problems with the bottle caps.

Assessment   Teacher will informally observe students' ability to count and to demonstrate understanding of regrouping by illustrating problems with bottle caps.

Human Bar Graph

Grade Level	3–5
Related Subject	Social studies
Materials	• Assorted pieces of colored construction paper, 9" x 9"
	• Staples, pins, glue, or tape
	• Large bulletin board or wall space
	• Graph paper
	• Colored pencils
Objectives	• Students will collect and graph data.
	• Students will recognize and use the appropriate parts of a graph.

Procedure   Before class make a large grid on a bulletin board or wall. Make the squares of the grid the same size as the pieces of construction paper you will use. (You might use 9" x 9" squares, but they could be smaller if you do not have a large space to use.) Write the months of the year on the horizontal axis. Number 1 through 10 on the vertical axis of the grid; you can number beyond 10, if needed.

Assign a different color to each month. Cut several squares (approximately 3" x 3") of construction paper in each of these colors. Next, on the board make a chart of the months and the numbers of students with birthdays in each of the months. Then, give each student a colored square of construction paper that corresponds in color to his or her birth month.

Have the students, one at a time, put their square of construction paper on the graph above their birth month, beginning at 1. This will create a bar graph. Discuss the data with the students. Which month has the most birthdays? Which has the least? Is there a month in which no one in the class has a birthday? (The discussion could be extended to discuss special holidays in each month, weather during various months, and more.) Have students discuss and choose an appropriate title for the graph. Discuss the horizontal axis and vertical axis and students' roles in graphing this information.

Next, have students each take a piece of graph paper and colored pencils and recreate the larger graph on their paper. Then brainstorm with the class other things on which they could collect data and graph. Have each student choose a different topic and create an original bar graph. Data should be information that can be collected from the class. Some examples are height of students in inches, number of siblings, favorite color, favorite beverage, favorite television show, and favorite school subject.

Assessment   Students' original graphs will be assessed for understanding of the components that make up a complete bar graph.

Cookin' With Fractions

Grade Level	6–8
Related Subjects	Home economics, social studies
Materials	• Paper and pencils
	• Recipe
	• Ingredients for recipe
	• Measuring spoons and cups
	• 13" x 9" x 2" pan
Objectives	• Students will use addition and multiplication of fractions to calculate how to double or triple a recipe.
	• Students will measure ingredients and follow recipe directions.
	• Students will work cooperatively to prepare a recipe.

Procedure   Any recipe can be used for this lesson. However, you might use a simple no-bake cookie recipe to allow students the experience of creating without the necessity of having oven facilities available to use. Whichever recipe you choose, students will enjoy this activity. Ask parents to provide the ingredients, or perhaps appeal to the parent council for monetary assistance.

Provide copies of the recipe for each student. Then have the students perform the needed mathematical calculations for doubling or tripling the recipe. You can go as far as you want with this, even asking them to figure out the amount of ingredients that would be needed if this particular recipe were to be served to the entire school.

Decide the quantity you will prepare in class, and have students figure out the total amount of ingredients needed. When it comes time to prepare the recipe, it might be best to have several small groups working with the original quantities—thus you will have three or four batches, rather than one huge batch.

If you have kitchen facilities where recipes can be prepared, it might be fun to have students bring favorite recipes from home, or research recipes to prepare from other countries. If you are limited in space and resources, try this simple no-bake cookie recipe:

No-Bake Chocolate Cookie Bars

1/4 c. butter or margarine, melted
1/2 c. white corn syrup
2/3 c. cocoa
1 c. sifted confectioner's sugar

Dash salt
1 c. coarsely chopped nuts
2/3 c. flaked coconut (optional)
6 oz. (4 1/2 c.) cereal
    (puffed wheat, corn flakes or
    crisped rice)

In large bowl, blend butter with corn syrup, cocoa, sugar, and salt. Add nuts, coconut, and cereal. Stir mixture until cereal is well coated. Pack this mixture firmly into greased 13" x 9" x 2" pan. Refrigerate several hours or until firm. Cut into squares. Makes 3–4 dozen.

Assessment   Students' calculations will be checked for accuracy. Students may also assess their own abilities to work cooperatively in a group to prepare the recipe.

It's Cool in the Pool

Grade Level	6–8, 9–12
Related Subjects	Chemistry, economics, language arts
Materials	• Paper and pencils
	• Calculators
	• Meter sticks
	• Access to a swimming pool
Objectives	• Students will calculate the number of gallons of water required to fill a swimming pool.
	• Students will calculate the amount of chemicals that must be added to the water for sanitation.
	• Students will project the estimated cost of operating a swimming pool for a given season.
	• Students will write a position paper for or against having a public swimming pool in their area (or school).

Procedure   If your high school has a swimming pool, you will need to schedule a time to take your class to the pool to take measurements. If not, schedule a trip to a nearby public pool. This can even be done off-season.

First, have students calculate the total gallonage of the pool. For a rectangular pool, the formula is Length x Width x Average Depth x 7.5 = gallonage. You will need to estimate the average depth. If the pool goes from 3–10 feet, a good guess at average depth would be 5.5 feet. Have students use meter sticks to take measurements.

Second, ask the pool caretaker about how the pool is sanitized and what chemicals are routinely added to the pool. Ask what factors influence how much sanitizer is needed (i.e., bather load and weather for an outdoor pool). Have the caretaker demonstrate how the pool is tested for chlorine and pH levels. Have students estimate the amount of chemicals that would be needed to keep the pool in operation for an entire season.

Third, have students contact a local pool supply store to find the cost of the needed chemicals. Based on their previous calculations, have students estimate the total cost of pool chemicals for one season.

Fourth, have students brainstorm a list of other expenses that may be incurred such as lifeguards, management, cleaning, repairs, etc. Also, have them list the current or possible uses of the facility.

Lastly, given all this information, have students prepare a position paper either in favor of or against the continued maintenance and upkeep of the pool. If they support the pool, they will need to make a case for the recreational and physical fitness benefits of the pool. If they do not support the expenditure of public funds for a swimming pool, they will need to cite the costs involved and give supporting evidence of why this is not the best use of public funds.

Assessment   The students' position papers will be evaluated to assess their level of understanding of the expenses involved in the operation of a swimming pool. The teacher will informally assess their calculations as the class works together to collect the necessary data in order to determine total expenses.

CHAPTER 9
SCIENCE

Button, Button—Who Has the Button?

Grade Level   K–2

Related Subject   Art

Materials
- Large box of buttons, at least 15 per student
- Rectangular pieces of cardboard
- Glue

Objectives
- Students will classify objects according to a dichotomous classification scheme.
- Students will create an original piece of artwork given materials provided.

Procedure   Divide the box of buttons so that each student has at least 15. Then ask students to divide their buttons in half, using criteria of their choosing. The important thing is that the buttons are approximately divided in half. (One student may put white buttons in one half and colored buttons in the other half. Another student may put large buttons in one half and small buttons in the other half.) Discuss the various ways students chose to divide their buttons. Depending on the age of the students, you may want to have them draw a diagram of their classification scheme.

Now see if the students can establish criteria to further divide the buttons into four parts. For example, if the first division was white and nonwhite, then the white buttons might be divided by size and the nonwhite buttons by one-color or multicolor.

The idea in a dichotomous classification scheme is to keep dividing the items approximately in half each time until each item is in a class by itself. With younger students it might be better to just divide twice and then discuss the traits that were used to decide in which group each button belonged.

When sufficient time has been given to classification, allow students to create an original piece of art on the cardboard pieces by gluing the buttons onto the cardboard. If desired, you could provide other materials for students to add to their pictures, such as pipe cleaners, material scraps, or fabric trim.

Assessment   Teacher will informally observe the students' dichotomous classification schemes to assure that they understand the concept of traits. Each piece of artwork may be self-assessed by students.

Mmmm, Mmmm Good!

Grade Level	3–5
Related Subject	Mathematics
Materials	• One regular-sized package M & Ms
	• One Fun Size package of M & Ms for each student (available around Halloween)
	• Graph paper for each student
Objectives	• Students will predict how many pieces of candy of each color will be in a package.
	• Students will collect and record data.
	• Students will compute a class average using the class data.
	• Students will create and correctly label a graph of their data.

Procedure   Ask students to predict how many M & Ms of each color will be in the regular-sized package. Write their predictions on the board. Open the package and group the candies by colors (use an overhead projector if possible). Demonstrate how a bar graph or circle graph could be made of the data.

Give students one fun-sized package each of M & Ms. Ask them to predict how many pieces of candy of each color will be in their packages, and record their predictions. Have students open their packages and count and record actual numbers of each color. Compare actual results to their predictions. Make a table on the board of each student's results to form a class total, and then use that information to computer a class average.

Have students construct graphs, both of their own data and of the class average. Remind students that graphs need to have a title and be clearly labeled.

Optional   Conduct an experiment by having each student place one piece of candy in his or her mouth at the same time. Without any chewing or manipulating of the candy, how long does it take for the candy to melt in their mouths? Hypothesize why some candies melted faster than others.

When all experiments are finished and data is recorded, eat the rest of the candy and enjoy!

Assessment　　Students' graphs will be assessed according to accuracy, completeness, and neatness.

Study Plots

Grade Level	3–5, 6–8
Related Subjects	Language arts, mathematics, art
Materials	• Meter sticks
	• Several yards of cord, string, or twine
	• Paper and pencils for each student
	• Clipboard for each student
	• Art paper and supplies
	• Classified section of newspaper
Objectives	• Students will measure a circle with a 1-meter diameter.
	• Students will make and record observations.
	• Students will write a poem about a particular natural area, highlighting the unique aspects of the area.
	• Students will write a classified advertisement modeled after ads found in the local newspaper.

Procedure   Find a spot on the school grounds, or in an adjacent field or park, where students can spread out and each find a circular plot of land approximately one meter in diameter. Have students cut a piece of twine or string 1 meter in length. When students have found their spot, they will use the string to measure the boundaries of their study plot. Students should be advised to choose a spot with some unique characteristic, such as a tree, that will help them identify their plot on future visits.

Using the clipboard students will make observations of their plot and record all of the observations they make. A diagram of identifying features would also help students find their plot the next time the class goes to study the plots.

Students should visit their study plots several times throughout the year and each time record any changes they notice; i.e., things changed as a result of the seasonal changes and the effects of human intervention on the plot.

On the second or third visit, have students sit quietly in their plots and use all of their senses to make observations. Then have them write a poem about their study plots, including as many identifying characteristics as possible.

Have students create a picture of their study plot. See if others can identify their plot from the drawings.

Near the end of the school year or semester, have students study classified ads in the newspaper and then write an ad to sell their plot. Students should use their imaginations and be creative with their ads. (Example: *Must move—family has grown and tree is no longer large enough to accommodate our needs. Mature maple tree in spacious 1-meter diameter plot near elementary school. 25 acorns or best offer. Reply to Joe Squirrel, c/o this paper.*)

Assessment   Students' field notes will be evaluated with each visit to the study plots. Poems, drawings, and classified ads will be evaluated for accuracy, completeness, and creativity.

Paper Making

Grade Level	6–8, 9–12
Related Subjects	Art, language arts
Materials	• Old paper (NOT newspaper)
	• Old blender (used only for papermaking)
	• Dishpan
	• Piece of screen, edged with duct tape, smaller than dishpan
	• Large bowl
	• Newspaper (lots)
	• Hot water
	• Cornstarch
	• Large sheet of vinyl or plastic to cover carpet
	• Sponges
Source	Kristin Brier, *Teacher's Garbage Gazette,* Wildcat Creek Solid Waste District, Lafayette, IN
Objectives	• Students will demonstrate the process used in recycling paper products.
	• Students will form an assembly line and work cooperatively to complete the recycling process.

Procedure   Set up stations around the room where each step of the recycling process will be completed. Explain the entire process to the class and then assign students to perform the various steps. Explain that this is the assembly-line concept where each worker does one specific job and the product is moved down the line.

Tear old paper into small pieces and put it in the bowl. Add hot water and let it soak for a few minutes. Fill the blender about half full of the wet paper and add more hot water until the blender is about two-thirds full. Add a few small pieces of colored construction paper to your recycled paper to add color.

Blend the mixture until it is pulpy; this is called pulping. (The paper fiber and water mixture is called a slurry.) Mix in about 1 teaspoon of starch, if desired, for stiffer paper.

Pour the slurry into the dishpan. Slide the screen into the bottom of the dishpan, and move it around until it is evenly covered with paper pulp.

Lift the screen out carefully, holding it level. Hold it steady, allowing it to drain for about one minute.

Put the screen, pulp side up, inside a piece of folded newspaper. Close the newspaper over the screen and pulp, then flip it over so that the screen is on top of the pulp.

Place a board or large book over the paper and have students stand on it. This process, which squeezes the water out of the paper, is called couching. Soak up the excess water with the sponges.

Open the newspaper and peel the screen off the top of the new piece of recycled paper. Let the new paper dry for a day or two. Use a hairdryer to speed up the drying process.

The new paper can be used for an art project or a writing lesson.

Assessment   Students' abilities to work together cooperatively will be informally assessed by the teacher throughout the project. Students will self-assess the success of the project by judging quality of paper and by completing a checklist.

CHAPTER 10
HEALTH

Growing Like a Weed!

Grade Level	K–2
Related Subjects	Social studies, language arts
Materials	• Baby pictures of each student (supplied by parents)
	• Several small mirrors (one per student, if possible)
	• Paper
	• Pencils and crayons
Objectives	• Students will recognize that they are growing and changing.
	• Students will create self-portraits at various stages of their lives.

Procedure   Early in the school year, ask students' parents to provide a baby picture of their child. Display the pictures in the front of the room, and ask the students to identify each baby.

Hold a class discussion in which students brainstorm a list of things that they can do now but could not do when they were babies. Then ask those students who have older siblings whether there are things the older siblings can do that they cannot do. Make a list of things that the students will be able to do when they are older but cannot do now.

Give each student his or her baby picture and a mirror (or a copy of the current school picture). Have each student fold a large piece of drawing paper into thirds. On the middle third, have them draw a self-portrait at their present age. On the left third, have them draw a picture of what they looked like as a baby, using the baby photo as a guide. On the right third, have them draw what they think they might look like when they grow up. Have the students write a caption for each picture, such as, "When I was a baby, I could smile and coo. Now I can read and write. When I grow up, I will have a job."

46

Assessment   The students should self-assess their art work.   The teacher will assess students' understanding of the concept of growing and changing by reading the students' captions.

"Colds 101" Research Activity

Grade Level	3–5, 6–8
Related Subject	Mathematics
Materials	• Sink
	• Paper towels
	• Water
	• Hand soap
	• Vaseline (baby powder scent)
	• Glitter (colored)
	• Pencil
	• Watch
Source	Karen Miller, West Lafayette, Indiana
Objectives	• Students will describe how germs are spread through direct contact.
	• Students will demonstrate proper hand-washing techniques to stop the spread of germs.

Procedure   Thoroughly stir a small amount of glitter into a jar of Vaseline. Divide the Vaseline into 1- to 2-tablespoon portions, placing each in a small Ziploc bag for each student.

Hold a class discussion about how germs spread through direct contact. Tell students that their homework will be to do some research involving members of their families.

Give students a worksheet with the following instructions:

Put a small dab of glitter Vaseline on your finger, and spread it all over your hands. Shake hands with someone in your family. Record below what happens.

If you had a cold, what would the glitter represent?

What happens when you have a cold, blow your nose, and touch someone else?

Perform actions A.–D. below, and record the time it takes for glitter to fully disappear in each instance. Remember to apply a little Vaseline to your hands before each procedure.

Number of Seconds until
All Glitter Disappears

A. *Wipe hands with paper towels*   _____
B. *Wash hands in* <u>*cold*</u> *water.*   _____
C. *Wash hands in* <u>*warm*</u> *water.*   _____
D. *Wash hands in* <u>*soapy*</u> *water.*   _____

Which procedure worked best to get rid of glitter?

Why do you think so?

What have you learned about the spread of germs?

After students conduct the experiments at home, have them make a bar or line graph of their data. Next, have students share the data to compute a class average, then graph that data.

Assessment   Students' individual and class composite graphs will be assessed for accuracy, completeness and neatness.

Cereal Box Unit

Grade Level   3–5, 6–8

Related Subjects   Language arts, economics, consumer science

Materials
- Empty cereal box for each student
- Assortment of construction paper
- Glue
- Scissors
- Markers, crayons, etc.

Objectives
- Students will recognize and use effective advertising techniques.
- Students will learn the sections of a cereal box that are required by law.
- Students will evaluate cereals based on a variety of data, such as nutritional value, value for the cost, and taste.

Procedure   Have students bring in a variety of empty cereal boxes. (Supply a few for the students who may not be able to do so.) As part of your unit on nutrition, have students analyze the ingredients, nutrients, Percent Daily Values, and related information. Rank the various brands of cereal by vitamins, calories, dietary fiber, additives, taste, and similar items. How does the cereal with the best overall nutritional ranking rate in popularity?

Discuss advertising techniques. Have students share any TV advertising they have seen and heard about any of these cereals. Ask students if they feel persuaded by these ads to try new cereals. Look at cereal boxes. What advertising techniques are used on the boxes? Are they effective?

How does price figure into consumer behavior when it comes to buying cereal? Have students compare some of the brands' prices. Also ask them to check if the grocery shopper in their family considers price when shopping for cereal.

After the study of nutrition and advertising techniques, tell students to create their own brand of cereal. Take an empty cereal box and cover it with construction paper. Then decorate it to reflect the characteristics of the cereal that was "invented." Remind students that they must list ingredients and nutrition facts. They should try to be as creative as possible in designing the cereal box.

Students will then write a sixty-second commercial featuring their new cereal creation. They will perform this commercial, which the teacher will videotape.

Assessment   Students' cereal box creations will be assessed for attention to detail in listing government-required components of food labels. Students' use of various advertising techniques and creativity will be assessed by the teacher through cereal box creations. Peer assessment on commercials and cereal boxes will also be used.

Are You a Junk Food Junkie? *or* Where's the Grease?

Grade Level	9–12
Related Subject	Consumer science
Materials	• Assorted snack foods
	• Paper towels
Objective	When presented with nutritional information, students will choose snacks lower in fat.

Procedure   Ask students to bring to class a regular-sized serving of their favorite snack food (i.e., potato chips, etc.). Give every student a paper towel and have them write their name on one corner. Then have them put their snack, without any wrapping, on the paper towel. Place the paper towels in an area of the classroom where they will be safe overnight.

The next day, have students look at their paper towels to see how much grease has been absorbed from their snack food. Lead a class discussion about the various types of foods that were tested. Were there any surprises? Ask students if this experiment might change their minds when choosing a snack food in the future.

Extension   An extension of this lesson would be to ask students to obtain nutrition information at various fast-food restaurants they may frequent. (Or, you could go to the various restaurants and collect these yourself.) Bring the information to class and compare the calories and fat content of the various fast-food meals. Compare this data to the amount of calories that the students, based on their age and size, should consume to maintain a healthy weight. Also, compare the percentage of fat calories that the fast-food meals contain to the recommended amount of fat calories in a daily diet.

Assessment   Students should be presented with several menus and asked to select the menu that would seem to be lowest in fat.

CHAPTER 11
SOCIAL STUDIES

Playing Store

Grade Level	K–2, 3–5
Related Subject	Mathematics
Materials	• A wide variety of empty containers of objects typically purchased at the grocery store (cereal, canned goods, detergent bottles, condiments, etc.)
	• Grocery sacks, one per student
	• Play money
	• Adding machine, toy cash register, or calculator
Objectives	• The students will make consumer choices in a simulated shopping scenario.
	• The students will estimate totals for a group of items.
	• The students will plan spending to fit within a budget.

Procedure   This is a lesson that can easily be adapted from kindergarten all the way through elementary school and perhaps even middle school.

Collect a wide variety of containers from food items and other items typically purchased at the grocery store. Enlist parents to help you collect these containers. Be sure to thoroughly rinse bottles and take care to remove rough edges from cans. Leave all labels intact.

Arrange the containers in a display in a corner of your classroom to simulate a grocery store. Allow the students to practice being consumers by choosing the items they will purchase.

Tell younger students the total number of items they may purchase. Have students take turns playing the role of cashier, ringing up sales on a toy cash register. After students make their choices, discuss why they chose those particular items.

As students begin to learn more math, see if you can find an old-fashioned adding machine that uses tape. Put prices on the items and add up students' purchases. As they are able to begin to estimate, perhaps give them a total that they must not exceed when shopping.

For older students, explain that they must stay within a budget. Then tell them they will need to purchase all of the food and cleaning supplies they will need for one week. Have them estimate their total purchase before it is calculated on the adding machine. Perhaps give a prize to the student whose estimate comes closest to the actual total.

Assessment   The teacher may informally assess younger students as they role-play shopping. Older students may be assessed by comparing their estimates with actual totals.

Medieval Castles

Grade Level	3–5, 6–8
Related Subjects	Reading, art, mathematics
Materials	• Books containing pictures of castles (suggest *Castle* by MacCauley)
	• A variety of cardboard and plastic object collected by students and teacher
	• Tempera paint, markers
	• Scissors
	• Glue
	• Other miscellaneous art supplies
	• Graph paper
Objective	Students will construct models of castles with realistic features, according to pictures found in picture books.

Procedure   This is the perfect culminating activity for a unit on the Middle Ages. Divide students into groups of four or five students. Using recycled materials such as cardboard, plastic, and tin or aluminum, have the students plan and construct a model castle. You may provide all the materials, giving each group identical materials with which to work, or the students may bring items from home.

Allow students class time to draw plans for the castle on graph paper and to actually construct it. Encourage them to include authentic-looking features in their plans, such as drawbridges that work. Students should consult books for ideas.

Assessment   Have an impartial third party (perhaps another teacher or the principal) judge the castles, looking for proper scale and attention to detail. Teacher observation and group self-evaluation can be used to assess how the group used teamwork to accomplish its goal.

We Are the World

Grade Level   6–8, 9–12
Related Subjects   Mathematics, language, health
Materials   • One envelope for each student
                     • Play money, bills and coins
                     • Individually wrapped candy
                     • Notes in English and Spanish for each student
                     • Red pen or marker
Source   Karen Russell, Columbus North High School, Columbus, Indiana
Objectives   • Students will verbally express their reactions to the conditions of the world regarding illiteracy, homelessness, hunger, and poverty.
                     • The students will calculate percentages.

Procedure   Before beginning your preparation, keep the following statistics about world conditions in mind. You will write this information on the board later.

Illiteracy   70% of world population cannot read
Homelessness   60% of world population has substandard or no housing
Hunger   50% of world population has insufficient food for proper nutrition
Poverty   6% of world population controls half or more of the wealth

Prepare an envelope for each student, as follows:

1. Using the percentages above, calculate the number of students in your class population "experiencing" each of the world conditions. (For example, a class of 28 students would have 20 illiterate students, 17 homeless students, 14 students suffering from insufficient food, and 2 students controlling the wealth.)
2. Use the numbers you determined in step 1 to symbolize class representation of the world conditions, as follows:

a. **Illiteracy:** Insert a note in Spanish (or another language) in the envelopes (20 in our example). The note should read: *La mayoria de ustedes no pueden leer esto porque esta escrito es en espanol. Hay mucha gente por todas partes del mundo que no saben leer ni siguiera una palabra escrita.*

Among the other envelopes, insert a note in English, reading: *Most of the class has a note that they can't read because it is in a foreign language. Many people in the world cannot read in any language.*

b. **Homelessness:** Mark a red dot on the outside of the envelopes (17 in our example).

c. **Insufficient food:** Insert a piece of candy in only half of the envelopes (14 in our example).

d. **Control of wealth:** Disperse the play-money bills in each envelope (2 in our example). Disperse the play-money coins among the other envelopes.

Seal each envelope. Then, write the statistical information on the board before beginning a class discussion on these world conditions. Lead a class discussion, explaining the information on the board. When students understand that these figures apply to the total world population, distribute the envelopes to the class.

Instruct students to open their envelopes. Then, ask them to look at the paper in their envelopes. Have them raise their hands if they cannot read the words. The class should record the number of raised hands; explain that this figure represents the number of students in the class who are illiterate.

Next, ask the students to stand if they have a red dot on the outside of their envelopes. The class should record the number of students standing; tell them that this figure represents the number of students in the class who are homeless. Tell the students who are standing to remain standing throughout the rest of the exercise.

Then, ask the students who have no candy in their envelopes to raise their hands. The class should record the number of raised hands again; tell the class that this figure represents the number of students in the class who suffer from insufficient food for proper nutrition. Allow the students who have candy to eat it now.

Finally, ask the students to raise their hands if they have play-money bills, not coins, in their envelopes. The class should record the number of raised hands; explain that this figure represents the number of students in the class who control the wealth.

Have students count the total number of students in the class. Then, using this figure and the other four figures they recorded, have them calculate the percentage of the class population that is illiterate, is homeless, suffers from insufficient food for proper nutrition, and controls the wealth. Their calculations should match the percentages you wrote on the board.

Explain that the goal of this project is to visualize the world's population—represented by class population—and the proportions of it experiencing these undesirable conditions. Allow students to express how they felt earlier when they could not read, had to stand, did not get candy, or had play coins instead of bills.

Assessment   The teacher will informally assess the students' understanding of the concepts through class discussion.

Cemetery Study

Grade Level	6–8, 9–12
Related Subjects	Literature, art, mathematics, science
Materials	• Survey sheets
	• Clipboards
	• Pencils
Source	Ron Stellhorn, Waterloo High School, Waterloo, Illinois
Objectives	• Students will conduct research on local history.
	• Students will gather data in an objective manner and will make inferences from the data.
	• Students will use the sampling method to estimate the total number of tombstones in the cemetery.
	• Students will use measurement skills to construct a map of the cemetery to scale.

Procedure   The study of a local cemetery can be a very interesting and inexpensive lesson for your students. Perhaps a cemetery is within walking distance of your school or is easily accessible by public transportation.

Before the visit, secure permission from the cemetery and from parents. Discuss proper cemetery etiquette with students. Also, visit the cemetery yourself before the visit to become familiar with it and to plan for the students' activities.

Depending on the age of your students and your purposes in conducting this activity, you may choose to make one visit to a cemetery or a series of visits. The following activities can be used with your students during their cemetery visit:

Genealogy: Students look for gravestones with same last names and construct a family history and family tree from the data.

Symbolism: Students sketch the various symbols and designs found on tombstones and speculate on the meaning of these symbols.

Epitaphs: Students collect various epitaphs, noting the different types—philosophical, religious, or biographical. Students can then write epitaphs for historical figures they are currently studying or for fictional characters.

Literature: Students use information from local newspaper files or county historical societies to write poems in the style of Edgar Lee Masters' *Spoon River Anthology.*

Mapping: Students measure and make a map of the cemetery using proper scale. Students can estimate the total number of markers in the cemetery by counting the markers in one area (sampling) and then multiplying this figure by the number of sections.

Classification: Students can develop a classification system after observing the various types of markers. Students can note the dates of the markers to see if they can make inferences regarding popular styles of markers at particular times in history (e.g., a certain type of material may have been scarce during a particular time in history.) Have students develop a time line that shows when particular types of markers were popular.

Art: Students can do gravestone rubbings to preserve the history they have discovered on their cemetery visit. Use masking tape to tape a piece of blank paper to the gravestone. Then use a crayon (with the paper removed) to rub slowly back and forth until the design appears on the paper. Remind students to be respectful and careful with any gravestones that appear to be fragile.

Survey: Divide students into groups of four or five. Assign each group to a predetermined area of the cemetery. Have each student collect data in their area on two males and two females from the following time periods: pre-1850, 1850–1890, 1890–1930, 1930–1970. Students should collect information on lifespan and any other pertinent information provided on the gravestone (month of death, cause of death, war veterans, fraternal organizations, ethnicity, etc.) Depending on the size of your class, you will obtain data on 300–500 individuals. After the data is compiled, students can make inferences based on the data.

Some questions the data may help students answer are:

- What was the average lifespan of people during specific historical periods?
- How did the lifespans of males compare to females?

- How did these averages compare to national averages?
- What was the ethnic makeup of the community? Did it change over time?
- Was there an unusual number of deaths in a specific year or cluster of years? What might have caused these deaths?
- Were any of the deaths associated with childbirth?
- Did people die more frequently during a particular season of the year?
- To what extent did people from this community participate in the various wars?
- What organizations (social, fraternal, religious, veterans, etc.) have existed in the community? Are any of these still active?
- Who were the leaders of the community?
- What were the most common symbols found on gravestones? What did these symbols mean?

Assessment Students use class data to construct a graph illustrating one type of information collected by the class. Students may also be presented with information and asked to make inferences on that data.

Map Scavenger Hunt

Grade Level　　　　3–Adult
Related Subjects　　Geography, reading
Materials
- A variety of maps, laminated
- Masking tape
- Scavenger hunt worksheets
- Pencils
- Clipboards (optional)

Objective　　　　　Students will read and interpret various types of maps.

Procedure　　　Collect and laminate a variety of maps (old maps are just as useful as current maps for this activity). Number each map. Post the maps in the room so they are easily visible to students. Look at each map carefully and choose one piece of information you would like students to discover on the map.

　　　　Using the information, create a scavenger hunt worksheet with questions the students must answer. Ask students to indicate on which map they found their answers.

　　　　You can make this activity as simple or challenging as you like, depending on the questions you ask. Students can work alone or in pairs to discover the answers to their questions. Tell them that each map contains the answer to one question. The object of the activity is to find all the correct answers in the shortest amount of time.

　　　　To encourage students to examine the maps closely and read all of the material in the borders, include questions on the worksheet to which the answers can be found only by carefully examining the maps.

　　　　For a larger scavenger hunt, several teachers could display maps in hallways where students usually pass and add more questions or even more than one worksheet.

　　　　Examples of questions that might be used follow.
- Through what bodies of water would an oil tanker pass going from Kuwait to Cairo? (Middle East map)
- List as many things as you can that are no longer correct as shown on the 1973–1974 world map. (1973–1974 world map)

- Your teacher's birthday is July 24 (Leo). Last summer, she was in Australia on her birthday. Was she able to see the constellation for her zodiac sign? (constellation map)
- Your mother is on a business trip in Tokyo. She said she would call home on your birthday, March 28, at 12 noon. You live in Chicago. What date and time should she place the call from Tokyo? (time zones map)
- The first lunar landing in 1969 was in the Sea of Tranquility. Is this in the Northern or Southern Hemisphere? (Moon surface map)

Assessment   Answers to the students' scavenger hunt worksheets will be assessed for accuracy. Teacher will informally assess students' problem-solving techniques as they carry out this activity.

Mystery Landforms

Grade Level	3–5
Related Subject	Mathematics
Materials	• Empty box with lid (e.g., copy paper box)
	• Grid paper
	• Straightened coat hanger
	• A variety of objects to fit inside box
	• Masking tape
	• Colored pencils
Source	Sheri Johnson, Happy Hollow Elementary, West Lafayette, Indiana
Objective	The students will predict the mystery landform by graphing data they collect.

Procedure   Put a variety of objects inside the box to represent various landforms. For example, a Frisbee might represent a plateau and an overturned bowl could be a mountain. Tape the objects to the bottom of the box so they will not shift while students collect data.

Put the lid on the box. Label a grid sheet A, B, C, etc., along the horizontal axis and 1, 2, 3, etc., along the vertical axis. (Each square on the grid can thus be labeled; e.g., A1, B17.) Glue the sheet to the top of the box lid. Punch a hole through the box in the middle of each square on the grid paper.

Straighten a coat hanger and mark intervals at each inch. Zero will represent sea level, so it should be the top mark on the hanger. (When the coat hanger is pushed through a hole in the box lid and goes all the way down to the "0" mark, the student will know that the landform is at sea level in that spot.)

Before beginning the activity, students should choose colors to correspond to the numbers; e.g., 0 = blue, 1 = green, 2 = yellow, 3 = orange, etc. Use colors that roughly correspond with the way maps are colored to show elevation. This will allow an easier transition to reading elevation maps.

Give each student a piece of grid paper. Have students take turns choosing a square to test with the coat hanger. If a student chooses square B3, for example, and the coat hanger goes into the box up to "2" before it is stopped by an object, then the students will color square B3 yellow on their grid papers. After several holes have been "tested," the students will be able to get an idea of what the landform(s) look(s) like by looking at their colored-in grid papers. When someone has figured out what the mystery landform is, he or she can make a guess.

At the end of the activity, take the lid off of the box and let the students look at the mystery landform(s). How closely do the grid papers that students colored resemble the actual form(s) in the box?

Extension Use a thin piece of paper to lay over students' colored grids and draw lines around each colored area (there may be several squares for each color, so draw lines around the entire section) to transfer for a contour map.

Assessment The teacher will collect the students' grid papers and compare them to the actual landform(s) in the box.

Storytelling

Grade Level	K–2
Related Subject	Social studies
Materials	• A variety of pictures from calendars, magazines, and books, showing people in various situations
	• Paper
	• Pencils
Objective	Students will interpret a picture and tell or write an original story based on the picture.

Procedure   Collect a variety of pictures from calendars, magazines, old textbooks, picture books, photographs, or postcards. The pictures should include people participating in some activity. Have each student choose one picture about which he or she will write a story.

The stories should have a beginning, where a problem is introduced; a middle, where the characters try to work out the problem; and an ending, where the problem is resolved. Make sure the students understand that the story must come to some sort of resolution.

Depending on the reading and writing level of the students, they may write their own stories or dictate them to the teacher (or older student). When everyone has finished writing, have students share their stories with each other in a big storytelling fest.

Assessment   Students' stories will be evaluated on whether or not the story they prepared corresponds to the picture they chose. The stories will be checked to be sure that they have a beginning, middle, and ending.

Make Mine PBJ!

Grade Level	3–5
Related Subjects	NA
Materials	• Peanut butter
	• Jelly
	• Loaf of bread
	• Knife
	• Paper towels
Objective	Students will demonstrate writing and following directions.

Procedure Ask parents to volunteer to provide jars of peanut butter or jelly or loaves of bread for a language activity.

Ask students if they like peanut butter and jelly sandwiches and if they know how to make them. For their language assignment, have students write the directions for making the sandwiches. Tell them to be very specific in giving directions.

Take one set of directions at a time and call the student up to the front of the room. Say, "I'm going to make a sandwich for you, according to your directions." Then proceed to make the sandwich. Be literal! If the student says, "Put the peanut butter on the bread," but doesn't say to open the jar, just set the jar of peanut butter on top of the bread. If the student does say to open the jar, but doesn't say to use a knife, just reach into the jar with your fingers and get some peanut butter to smear on the bread. If the student doesn't tell you precisely how to put the two pieces of bread together, put them together with peanut butter and jelly on the outside of the sandwich.

It helps if you review the directions beforehand, arranging them in order from least specific to most specific. In this way, the last set you read and follow will be nearly exact.

Even though you are carrying the idea of writing and reading directions to a ridiculous level, the students will enjoy this activity immensely. They will also understand the need to be clear and precise in their writing.

Assessment   The student who gets a properly made peanut butter and jelly sandwich will have reached the objective for this lesson. The teacher will assess students' instructions according to proper order of steps and degree of specificity.

Oh, What a Life!

Grade Level	6–8
Related Subject	Social studies
Materials	• Three-ring binder for each student
	• Plastic page protectors (optional)
	• Photographs from home
	• Assorted memorabilia
	• Computer access
Objectives	• Students will create their autobiographies, from birth to their present age.
	• Students will use word processing to write their autobiographical chapters.
	• Students will use a desktop publishing program to create dividers and special pages for their autobiographies.

Procedure   This activity could be spread over several weeks. Students will prepare autobiographies, from birth to their present age. Students should be encouraged to interview their parents and grandparents to find out as much as they can about their family backgrounds. They will also want to ask their parents to tell them things they remember about their babyhood and early childhood. Students may want to refer to baby books and family albums for information.

A few weeks before beginning this project, send a note home to parents. In the note, ask them to find time to help the students look for needed resources and obtain three-ring binders and page protectors. (Have a backup plan for students who cannot afford these things. A business partner could cover these costs for a child.)

At school, provide computer lab time for students to work on writing their chapters with a word processing program. Suggested chapters for the autobiography are: Family Background, Family Tree Chart, Birth to One Year, Babyhood (2–4 years), Kindergarten, Grade One, Grade Two, Grade Three, etc., Special Vacations, and Future Plans. Students should be encouraged to add any special chapters they feel will enhance their autobiographies, such as a feature article about a famous relative or a chapter on some special accomplishment or hobby.

In addition to the written chapters, students should include photographs with captions and special memorabilia from their childhood. This could include such things as report cards, ribbons, special awards, or schoolwork.

If possible, have students put all of their pages in plastic sheet protectors. This will provide a uniform look for the autobiography and allow keepsakes to be safely displayed.

Students can use a desktop publishing program to design dividers for each chapter of their autobiographies. They may also be able to design an attractive way to display their family tree by using the publishing program.

Plan a special day after the autobiographies are finished for parents to come in to view them. The parents will enjoy seeing the students' work, and students will enjoy sharing their autobiographies with one another.

Assessment   Students' autobiographies will be evaluated based on overall neatness and attractiveness; spelling, grammar, and punctuation of written sections; completeness; and creativity in adding special touches to their autobiographies.

Packaging Your Portfolio

Grade Level   9–12

Related Subjects   All subjects, depending on student interest and choices

Materials
- Access to research tools
- Art supplies as needed

Objectives
- Students will plan and create a portfolio exhibiting a semester of work.
- Students will use research tools (i.e., Internet, library books, encyclopedias, etc.).

Procedure   This lesson can be adapted to many different situations. For a semester-long project, have students create a portfolio of their work. If this is used for an English class, the primary focus of the work should be writing—essays, poetry, research papers, etc. However, space should also be reserved for items of the student's choosing, which could include creative work in other areas, such as art work, video production, or musical compositions.

Each student should choose a theme for his or her portfolio. They could choose a particular author (e.g., Lewis Carroll), genre (e.g., science fiction), or time period (e.g., the Renaissance). All items in the portfolio should relate in some way to that theme. Specify the number of items that must be in the portfolio, depending on the grade level and the amount of time devoted to this assignment. You might also specify types of items to be included: (1) one research piece (e.g., about Lewis Carroll's life, science fiction in general, or the Renaissance), (2) one piece of original poetry about the topic, (3) one piece written in the appropriate style (e.g., a story in Lewis Carroll's style, a science fiction story, a story in the language and style of the Renaissance), and (4) other creative pieces chosen by the student.

Besides choosing a topic and the pieces to go in the portfolio, the student will also devise a creative way to package the portfolio components. Here is an example: One student chose Lewis Carroll as her subject. She read a biography and wrote her research piece on his life. She also read, among other works, *Alice in Wonderland*. From this story, she got the inspiration for her portfolio package. This package consisted of a cereal box, covered to look like an oversized box of playing cards. Inside the card box were several giant playing cards—all containing the Queen of Hearts on the back, a character in *Alice in Wonderland.* These cards were made by enlarging an actual playing card on a copy machine, then cutting two pieces of tagboard (could be old file folders) just the right size to fit into the box. On each side of the tagboard, she glued a copy of the playing card, colored by hand. The two pieces were laminated together and then a slit was made in the top of each card. The components of her portfolio were neatly tucked into the cards.

Assessment   The teacher will establish specific criteria as to the number and type of components required by the assignment. A rubric can be developed which takes into account the required components as well as the creativity exhibited in the final project.

CHAPTER 13
THINKING SKILLS

Students at all levels will benefit from activities that stretch their minds and encourage them to think in creative ways. Many books are available that offer creative-thinking exercises. With just a little imagination on your part, you can easily create your own creative thinking lessons. Here are some ideas to get you started.

Now You See It, Now You Don't

Grade Level	K–12
Related Subject	Science
Materials	• Small paper bag
	• Walnuts (or some other type of nut in a shell)
	• Nutcracker
Objective	Students will use clues to form hypotheses.

Procedure   Put the walnut in the paper bag. Place the nutcracker nearby, but out of sight from the students. Show students the paper bag and say, "Something is in this bag that no one has ever seen before. After I show it to you, no one will ever see it again. Can you guess what it is?"

Allow students time to offer guesses. When they have finished guessing, ask them if they would like to see what is in the bag.

Open the bag and remove the walnut. Use the nutcracker to crack open the nut. Hold up the nutmeat and say, "No one has ever seen this before." Now eat the nutmeat and say, "Now, no one will ever see it again!"

Assessment   The teacher will informally assess students' guesses to see whether they are using logical reasoning to form hypotheses.

How Many Ways Can You Use This?

Grade Level   K–12 (particularly popular with 3–8)
Related Subjects   Language arts; others depending on object chosen
Materials   Varied, see below
Objective   Students will list new ways to use familiar items.

Procedure   This is a great team-building activity for cooperative learning. It is fun to use at the start of the day to get things going, or in those awkward ten- to fifteen-minute time periods when you need a fill-in activity.

Have students work in pairs or groups of three or four. Give them a specific time limit, so this becomes a "rapid-fire" brainstorming activity.

Hold up a familiar item such as:
- A plastic ice cube tray
- An old shoe
- A muffin tin
- An old doorknob
- A paper grocery bag
- An empty milk carton

Tell students that they have five minutes (adjust to fit your schedule) to think of as many new creative uses for this item as possible. Have them write the ideas on a sheet of paper. At the end of the brainstorming time, reward the group that had the most uses. Have this group read aloud their list, so everyone can hear their ideas. This will help students to think more creatively next time.

As a variation, have the group with the most ideas read aloud their list. As they do, other groups will indicate by raising their hands if they had the *same i*dea. The object is to have an idea not common to any other group.

Students will begin to look forward to this activity if you use it at a predictable time each day (i.e., first thing in the morning, right after lunch, etc.) You can add to the list of items as you begin using this activity. In fact, coming up with a new item each day will cause you to do some creative thinking! You might ask students to bring in items or perhaps assign a specific student to bring in an item on a specific day.

Of course, on the day a student brings an item, that student will be excluded from the activity, since he or she would have lead time before class to begin thinking of uses for the item.

Assessment   The teacher will informally assess students' suggestions for creativity and viability. The teacher will also assess students' group skills to be sure they are allowing all students to participate and are displaying respectful attitudes concerning others' suggestions.

Memory Test

Grade Level	K–12
Related Subjects	Varied (depending on subjects to which objects relate)
Materials	Varied
Objective	Students will develop strategies for remembering a list of items or words.

Procedure   Bring in a box or tray containing ten items (use more for older students, fewer for younger students). The items may relate to each other in some way (e.g., items from your desk, kitchen utensils, art supplies, food items, etc.) Allow students one minute (less for older students, more for younger students) to study the items. Then remove them from the students' view. Have students write down all of the items they can recall; younger students can reply orally.

Discuss the strategies students used to help them remember the items.   Some students may have more fully developed memory strategies. It will be helpful for students to share their techniques.

As students get more proficient in this activity, the difficulty may be increased by adding more items, decreasing the time allowed, or choosing a group of items that are not related to each other in any way.

Assessment   The teacher will informally assess students' abilities to recall items. Through class discussion, the teacher will assess students' development of memory strategies.

Classification

Grade Level	3–12
Related Subjects	Science, language arts
Materials	• An assortment of small objects
	• Paper
	• Pencils
Objective	Students will classify objects according to a dichotomous classification scheme.

Procedure   Bring in an assortment of 10–12 small objects. You might want to have the objects related in some way. Later on, bring in objects that do not appear to be at all related.

Tell students to classify or group the objects. Have them discuss the objects and compare what is alike and what is different. Then, ask students to think of a classification scheme that would roughly divide the objects in half. For example, the items from a teacher's desk could include a stapler, tape dispenser, paper clip dispenser, pen, pencil, marker, family picture, bell, figurine, and a vase with a flower. One way of classifying these objects would be "those that do work" and "those that do not do work." In that case, the stapler, tape dispenser, paper clip dispenser, pen, pencil, and marker would go in the "those that do work" category and the rest would be in the "those that do not do work" category. To further classify, we could look at the "those that do work" category and divide them by "those that hold things together" (stapler, tape, paper clips) and "those that do not hold things together."

Draw a diagram on the board that shows the divisions and categories as the students find ways to divide or classify the objects. The idea is to continue subdividing each category until each item is in a class by itself.

Once the students have an idea of how dichotomous classification works, present them with another set of objects. This time, have them work in pairs to categorize the objects. When all students have finished, have them share their classification schemes. Did students find different ways to categorize the objects? There will probably be more than one way to classify them.

To further practice this skill, ask a student each day for the next few days to bring in a set of items for the other students to classify.

Assessment   The   teacher   will   informally   assess   students' understanding of a dichotomous classification scheme by listening to their explanations of how they chose to categorize objects.

PART III

ELECTRONIC AND OTHER RESOURCES

Professional organizations, special state departments (including departments of education), and public utility companies can provide materials and information useful for teachers. Their journals, books, videos, and other media can provide information or material that will help you teach creatively and generate ideas.

A large number of resources, including those just mentioned, also have Web sites. Many are related to specific subject areas. Be sure to browse these sites for more teaching material—right at your fingertips.

CHAPTER 14
PROFESSIONAL ORGANIZATIONS

Many subject area-specific professional organizations can help you locate free or inexpensive materials for teaching. These organizations often publish their own professional journals and periodicals that include suggestions to help you get started.

International Reading Association

800 Barksdale Road, P.O. Box 8139
Newark, DE 19714
http://www.ira.org

The International Reading Association Web site includes information on upcoming conferences and about the organization's publications. An online bookstore provides parents and professionals with information about ordering current titles.

National Council of Teachers of English

1111 West Kenyon Road
Urbana, IL 61801
http://www.ncte.org

The National Council of Teachers of English Web site includes information on conventions, grant opportunities, books, journals, and professional development. It also provides chat rooms where teachers can share views of various subjects related to reading. Teaching ideas are available on a variety of topics and grade levels.

National Council of Teachers of Mathematics

1906 Association Drive
Reston, VA 22091
http://www.nctm.org

This Web site offers online publications, meeting notices, professional development opportunities, a catalog, and WebNews. In addition, there is a classified advertising section where announcements of math workshops, conferences, and grants can be listed and math products are offered for sale.

National Council for the Social Studies

3501 Newark Street, NW
Washington, DC 20016
http://www.ncss.org

This Web site gives information on conferences, awards, grant opportunities, journals, publications, professional development opportunities, National Standards, and curriculum. There is also a discussion board. The site offers Internet links and resources. Teaching resources are organized by the Ten Themes of Social Studies and include such items as books, periodicals, CD-ROMs, units, games, electronic media, and videos.

National Research Council, National Academy of Sciences

2101 Constitution Avenue, NW, HA 450
Washington, DC 20418
http://www.nas.edu/nrc

The National Research Council Web site provides access to hundreds of scientific resources. The resources include links to the Aeronautics and

Space Engineering Board, Arts in the Academy, Board on Agriculture, Board of Atmospheric Sciences and Climate, Board on Biology, Board on Children, Youth and Families, Board on Earth Sciences, and many others.

The National Research Council library is also available online as a virtual library providing access to databases, documents, newspapers, a reference desk, government information, science and technology resources, and electronic journals. Virtually all journals in science and medicine are available online with a table of contents, article abstracts, and complete versions of selected articles.

CHAPTER 15
STATE DEPARTMENTS

Special Departments

Every state has a Web site that can take you to almost anywhere in the state. By linking up with your state's **Department of Natural Resources**, you can find information on state museums, historic sites, parks, reservoirs, and nature preserves. Information on the state's fish and wildlife as well as historic preservation and archaeology projects is also available. The state's **Department of Tourism** provides information on festivals and events throughout the state. State maps, photo galleries, and even travel pack information can be accessed through this link.

Every state's Web site will be unique to that state, and some are more extensive than others. To connect to your state's Web site, substitute your state's two-letter abbreviation for *in* in the following Web address:

http://www.state.in.us/

Departments of Education

Each state Department of Education also offers a Web site with many resources for teachers. The sites will provide links to other schools and services for teachers. Chat sites and Teachers' Lounge features allow teachers to communicate with each other and share ideas.

Use the Indiana Web site to link to all other states. The address for this site is:

http://www.ideanet.doe.state.in.us

You may also reach the U.S. Department of Education at:

http://www.ed.gov

CHAPTER 16
PUBLIC UTILITY COMPANIES

Your local public utility companies offer many educational resources for teachers. Check with them to see what is available in your area, and know that supplies may be limited.

You will find resources for all grade levels, from speakers to visit your classroom to science demonstrations, videos, slide programs, books, posters, software, CD-ROMs, and complete curriculum packets. Utility companies also sponsor contests for students and grant opportunities for teachers.

CHAPTER 17
WEB SITES

Many Web sites are available of interest to both students and teachers, but it is impossible to list them all. Several are listed here that offer great resources for the classroom.

Art and Photography

http://www.nga.gov

This Web site lends itself well to a virtual field trip. Students are able to view artwork that is on display in the National Gallery of Art. They may search by country, time period, or artist. This is definitely a site to bookmark.

http://www.nationalgeographic.com/media/photography

For generations, the National Geographic Society has taken us around the world and given us a glimpse of unusual cultures, religions, events, and places. This collection of the world's most famous photography will be enjoyed by all and may be of particular interest to aspiring young photographers. A feature of this site, the Camera Bag, gives students tips from the experts to help them become world-class photographers.

http://www.psilakis.gr

The amazing photography of Yannis Psilakis will take students to the remote corners of the earth where they will meet people from endangered cultures. They will meet the Hunzakut people of northern Pakistan and the Bolivian Aymara Indians and find themselves in the jungles of the Amazon and the fields of Ethiopia. This site offers a glimpse at some unique cultures that are quickly disappearing.

Current Events

http://www.abcnews.com

This site will put current events at students' fingertips. Links to special sections will lead, for example, to the latest medical research news in the Living section or to interactive time lines, maps, and media clips of the area of the world experiencing the latest political crisis in the World section. Background information will provide the context and bigger picture needed to help students (and teachers) to understand present world struggles.

http://www.nbc.com

NBC's Web site provides the television schedule, information on how to obtain tickets to NBC programs, and information on upcoming Specials. The news and information is divided into NBC Asia, NBC Europe, MSNBC Sports, and CNBC. Information about contests and games in which viewers can participate are also available at this site.

Free Software and More

http://www.thefreesite.com

Students who want to experiment with developing their own Web sites will enjoy going to this site. It allows students the opportunity to set up home pages for no charge, get free e-mail accounts, and also download free counters and graphics to use on their Web sites.

http://www.beyond.com

This site reviews many pieces of computer software that are free after sending for the rebates. Some of the items offered are Microsoft Encarta 99, Mission Force: Cyberstorm2, Vector ClipArt, Casper Brainy Books, and the Lords Royal Collection. You may order online.

http://www.jumbo.com

Over 300,000 shareware and freeware programs are available at this site for download.

Geography

http://www.nationalgeographic.com/kids

This site offers so much for students to enjoy that they will want to spend hours here. *National Geographic World Online* has many articles and activities for students to explore. They can discover Amazing Facts, find a pen pal in the Pen Pal Network, make cartoons at the Cartoon Factory, play the Name Game, or offer their own opinions on issues at the Kids Network. Links to arts and entertainment, television programs, and literature to supplement National Geographic's year-long theme are provided.

http://www.epa.gov/oppeoee1

This site on global warming by the Environmental Protection Agency gives students all the facts they need to understand what the greenhouse effect is doing to the earth's atmosphere. Forecasts take students to the future of our deserts, coastal zones, farms, and national forests. The site helps students discover what they can do to "turn down the heat" on this problem.

http://www.terraserver.microsoft.com

Aerial photographs, satellite images, and maps from around the globe can be found in this online database. Students can choose to visit any spot on Earth. Natural wonders like the Grand Canyon, ancient wonders like the Great Pyramids, or modern-day landmarks like Yankee Stadium can be viewed at this site.

History

http://www.historyplace.com

American history buffs are going to love The History Place. Historical photographs, documents, speeches, and time lines from the Civil War to the present day are all part of the archives available to students at this site. Students can also get assistance with their next research paper on the Homework Help page.

http://www.ioweb.com/civilwar

Documents, images, memoirs, and a diary of a Union soldier, Jefferson Moses, will give Civil War buffs the opportunity to immerse themselves in the war from this man's perspective. He reflects on the capturing of General Lee and the assassination of President Lincoln as well as his own experiences in Mississippi in the winter, the Yazoo Pass Expedition and the Battle of Vicksburg.

http://www.normandy.eb.com

The Invasion of Normandy during World War II is the subject of this Web site. Films of actual fighting, audiotapes of speeches, and biographies of leaders such as Churchill and Eisenhower are accessible through this site.

http://www.battle1066.com

Students will enjoy the feeling of a virtual time machine as they witness the clashing armor of the medieval Battle of Hastings. The Vikings, Romans, Saxons, and Normans all battle over the land that is now England. Students can visit the link for each group to learn its battle strategies. A reproduction of the famous Bayeaux Tapestry tells the story in hundreds of feet of needlework accompanied by a narration.

http://www.pbs.org/weta/faceofrussia

Students will get a comprehensive view of Russian culture as ten
centuries of Russian history are presented through art, music, dance,
architecture, and cinema. They will visit historic landmarks and meet
the personalities that shaped Russia throughout its fascinating history.
From the Russian Ballet to Sputnik, from Ivan the Terrible to Boris
Yeltsin, this is the Russian experience.

http://www.kultur.gov.tr/english/main-e.html

Become immersed in the culture of Turkey through the art, music,
architecture and history of this fascinating Old World country.
Landmarks such as the Derinkuyu Underground City, the Ruymeli
Fortress, and the Shah Nadir Throne await visitors. Get a glimpse of the
medieval bazaars, delicious kabobs, sacred mosques, as well as the
Turkish Ballet.

http://www.historyofindia.com

The mystique of the intriguing country of India is unveiled on this Web
site, from the beauty of the Taj Mahal to the bustling modern cities.
Step back in history and tour India through the visual time lines. Learn
about the rich culture and variety of this interesting country.

http://www.wl.k12.in.us.sstech

This Web site, developed by a social studies teacher and his students,
provides links to all sorts of social studies resources. The section on
Government takes you to government documents and offers links to the
various branches of government. A political dictionary and information
on elections is included. The Social Studies section is divided into
several categories, including World History, U.S. History, Economics,
Psychology, and Geography. Searches can become more specific by
selecting certain time periods or information on particular topics. This
site can "take you around the world" in your quest for social studies
information.

Research

http://www.classroom.com/staff/tmc/homewkk.htm

This site offers students help for getting organized in order to make the most of their study time and become efficient learners. It offers suggestions for how to use the Internet to help with homework.

http://www.homeworkcentral.com

This is a wonderful site that provides homework assistance for students from Grade 1 through college and beyond. It is easy to navigate, as students first choose their grade level and then the branch of study they wish to explore. The branches of study are divided into animals, arts, mathematics, biography, countries of the world, current events, geography, health and physical education, history, language arts, science, and social studies. Once students choose the branch, further divisions will take them to more specific information.

      The site also offers resources for teachers—lesson plans by subject and grade level and free software downloads. Information is also provided on school projects that students may participate in as well as on sources of free materials.

http://www.refdesk.com/facts.html

Just about every type of reference material students might need for any type of homework or project can be accessed through this site. A few of these are Acronyms, Atomic Clock, Calculator, Bartlett's Quotations, Biography, Comics, Roget's Thesaurus, Webster's Dictionary, Stock Quote, Maps, and People Search. One fun feature students will enjoy at the Comics site is the ability to send a comic to a friend via e-mail.

http://www.studyweb.com

This reference site covers many imaginable subject areas and allows students to continue to refine their searches. From science to grammar and art to mathematics, this site can provide so much information that students need.

http://www.state.ga.us

This will be a most useful Web site for students studying the states of the United States. This particular site will take you to the State of Georgia's home page, from which you can find out about the government, jobs, natural resources, schools, news, museums, and tourist attractions of the state. Then, by substituting any state's two-letter abbreviation for *ga* in the Web address, you can go to that state's official home page. Thus, you have basically been introduced to 50 new Web sites!

http://www.howstuffworks.com

This site provides an inside look at many everyday inventions in order to appeal to the engineer in everyone. Students can find out what makes many modern-day conveniences work, such as a microwave oven, telephone, smoke detector, tire gauge, internal combustion engine, or even a toilet. This site will be a favorite of any student who enjoys tinkering or who has ever just wondered how something works.

http://www.discovery.com/past/stories/moreinventors.html

This site will give students a good look at great inventions, both past and present. Stories of how inventors got their ideas will fascinate students. Students will learn about the invention of such things as the skateboard, the Frisbee, the first video game, and even a rocket belt (used by James Bond). Students will have lots of fun on this site.

Science

http://www.explorescience.com

On this site students and teachers are able to interact with materials on the Web, not just read science text. Many different experiments and games are available, divided into Mechanics, E & M, Life Sciences, Waves, Astro, Optics, Games, and Basics. This site offers all the fun and learning of science experiments with no cleanup.

http://www.insecta.com

This site gives students a chance to get up close and personal with bugs—without getting stung or bitten. From ladybugs to termites, cockroaches to butterflies, you'll find them all here. Students can view a magnified image of each insect. A glossary of terms and family trees of insect classes are included. Students will learn lots of fascinating facts about the insect world on this site.

http://www.pbs.org/wnet/savageearth

The science behind such natural phenomena as earthquakes, volcanoes, and tsunamis is revealed through animated X-ray views of these disasters. Students can ask questions and learn all about lava, tidal waves, and plate tectonics.

Space

http://www.exploratorium.edu/observatory

This fascinating site brings the world of outer space right to students' computer screens. There are many interactive exhibits and historical accounts to keep students interested and give them a better idea of what space is really like. Students will view X-ray images, magnetic fields, shooting stars, sunspots, and more. They will also learn something about the mythology surrounding the mysteries of the universe. This site also provides several links to other sites as well as a teacher's page with ideas for classroom use.

http://www.nasa.gov

Information on viewing a launch or visiting one of the NASA centers is included in the Web site, in addition to the history of the space program. Educational resources for teachers are available.

http://www.nationalgeographic.com/features/98/mars

This virtual reality tour allows students to experience the 1997 Pathfinder mission to Mars. They can view the Martian landscape, watch the Pathfinder's fiery landing on the planet, and take a virtual ride on the Sojourner, the first interplanetary land rover. The virtual adventure is complete when students are given the opportunity to send a postcard to friends from Mars via e-mail.

Sports

http://www.ultranet.com/~rhickok

This is a sports history site, not a sports news site. Sports buffs will find much to engage them at this site. This would be a great site for that reluctant student who is not interested in doing research but is interested in sports. In addition to the information the site provides, there is also an opportunity for students to interact by reading and posting messages. They may also create their own sports greeting cards to send to their friends via e-mail.

Stories

http://www.storiestogrowby.com

This is a great collection of stories from around the world. Students and teachers may search for a particular type of story: adventure, animal tales, fairy tales, kings and queens, and more. They may also look for a theme, such as cooperation, courage, creative thinking, or friendship. Stories are also listed by continent, country, or people of origin. After students read the stories, they can leave a message at the site about what they thought of the stories or even read what other kids have said about the stories.

Teacher Resources

http://www.pbs.org/teachersource

PBS has established this site to help teachers make the most of the PBS programming available to them. The TV schedule is available on this site as well as activities and lesson plans to accompany programs. Related sites that the students may wish to access are also listed. Copyright and taping information about educator-extended taping rights is included.

Teachers can search by key word in order to correlate the PBS programs to national and state standards in several states. Teachers may also request to receive weekly updates on PBS programming via e-mail.

Trivia

http://www.quizsite.com

If students enjoy *Jeopardy* and Trivial Pursuit, they'll love this site. Quiz questions on a wide variety of topics test their brain power. Students can even donate their favorite questions and take advantage of opportunities to win prizes.

http://www.altonweb.com/history/wadlow

If students love reading the *Guinness Book of World Records,* then this site will appeal to them. It tells the story of Robert Pershing Wadlow from Alton, Illinois. Wadlow is the tallest person in history, at a height of 8 feet 11 inches.

http://www.yakscorner.com

This cybermagazine for kids offers jokes, contests, crafts, games, interactive activities, news, and information for them to enjoy. Hosted by a big yak, this site offers much to entertain and inform students. The yak leads travelogues to various world locations and offers news of interest to kids.

REFERENCES AND SUGGESTED READINGS

Bernier, G., Burrows, K., Greeble, M., Hoffner, S., Perry L., and
Shapley, B. 1987. *Knowledge in Bloom.* West Palm Beach, FL:
Palm Beach Newspapers, Inc.

Brier, K. Fall, 1998. Making paper. *The Teacher's Garbage Gazette.*
Lafayette, IN: Wildcat Creek Solid Waste District.

Garrett, S. D., McCallum, S., and Yoder, M. 1997. *Newspapers:
Touching the Kaleidoscope of Your Mind.* Newark, DE:
International Reading Association.

Garrett, S. E., and Morrison, B. S. 1991. *Citizens Together.* Washington,
DC: American Newspaper Publishers Association Foundation.

Russell, K. November/December, 1991. If we were the world.
Indianapolis, IN: Geography Educators' Network of Indiana,
Inc.

Seidelman, J. E., and Mintonye, G. 1970. *Shopping Cart Art.* New
York: Collier Books.

WWW.4KIDS.ORG. Fall, 1998. *The Lafayette Journal and Courier,* p.
D6.